Published By Robert Corbin

@ Sean Turner

Dukan Diet Recipes: Easy Recipes for All Four Phases of the Dukan Diet

All Right RESERVED

ISBN 978-87-94477-38-3

TABLE OF CONTENTS

Black Eye Peas With Greens 1

Poultry Bacon Egg Sandwich 4

Oat Bran Muffins 6

Cheesy Chivey Eggs Attack 8

Shrimp Skewers With Lemon And Parsley 9

Chicken Salad With Celery And Mustard 12

Tofu Cubes Marinated In Spices 15

Egg And Onion Burin 18

Chocolate Oat Bran Cereal 19

Breakfast Frittata 22

Marinated Chicken Bites With Lemon Juice And Spices 24

Tuna Carpaccio With Olive Oil Olive Oil And Balsamic Vinegar 26

Egg And Tomato Muffins 28

Smooth And Creamy Cauliflower Mash 30

Warm Roasted Red Pepper And Cauliflower Pate ... 32

- Green Smoothie 33
- Classic Strawberry Smoothie 34
- Gobi Burr Muffins 35
- Crockpot Flank Steak 37
- Loaf Of Bread 39
- Pumpkin Soup 41
- Creamy Surimi Salad 43
- Barbequed Cod On Wilted Spinach 45
- The Ideal Cookie "One" According To Dukan 47
- Crunchy Biscuits "Simple" According To Dukan 50
- Khachaturian With A Boat In A Frying Pan According To Dukan 54
- Thai Chicken With Broccoli And Shirataki Noodles .. 57
- Shirataki Noodles With Balsamic Vinegar 61
- Thousand Inland Dressing 63
- Quinoa Salad With Cauliflower 65
- Baked Salmon Omelet 68
- Caraway Chops 70

Curettes And Fresh Cheese Omelets 72

Salmon Rolls With Asparagus 75

Greek Chicken Salad With Cucumbers And Olives ... 78

Mediterranean Chicken Drumsticks 81

Chicken Caesar Salad 83

Bristol With Arugula And Parmesan Shavings 84

Spinach Cudgel 86

Tender Grilled Venison 88

Spaghetti With Beef Broth 90

Chicken With Lemon And Capers 93

Cod With Mustard Sauce 95

Vietnamese Beef 97

Chicken Curry With Crunchy Vegetables 99

Garlic And Dill Chicken Breasts 103

Steak Au Pire 104

Grilled Vegetable Skewers 107

Guacamole With Celery Chips 109

Tofu And Veggie Stir Fry 111

Chilled Seafood Salad 113

Cardamom Tart.. 116

Apple Tart 117

Muesli Bars According To Dukan 119

Swordfish Carpaccio With Arugula And Lemon 124

Chicken Meatballs With Tomato Sauce 127

Chicken Supreme 131

Baked Egg Custard 133

Chicken Nuggets 135

Hard-Boiled Eggs Cut In Half And Seasoned With Herbs 137

Chocolate Ice Cream Dukan Style 139

Prawn Cocktail Dukan-Style 141

Black Eye Peas With Greens

Ingredients:

- 1/2 teaspoon smoky paprika or liquid smoke
- 1 tsp dried oregano
- 1/2 teaspoon dried thyme
- 1/2 teaspoon sea salt
- 1/4 teaspoon freshly ground black pepper
- 6 cups lowsodium vegetable broth
- 1 pound dry black eyed peas
- 1 cup yellow onion diced
- 3 cloves garlic minced
- 1 carrot peeled and diced

- 1 cup red bell pepper diced

- 2 cups chard spinach or collard greens, sliced (optional)

Directions:

1. Rinse peas under running water and remove any bad peas and small stones. Transfer to a medium saucepan.
2. Cover in water by at least 3 inches and soak for at least 6 hours to overnight. Drain and rinse beans under cold water.
3. To a large pot over medium heat add 1/4 cup water (or vegetable broth), diced onion, garlic, carrots, and bell pepper. Sauté, stirring occasionally, until the onions are translucent.
4. Add liquid smoke, oregano, salt, and pepper. Sauté a few more minutes.
5. Add drained beans and vegetable broth. Bring to a boil, reduce heat, and simmer, covered,

about 45 minutes or until beans are tender. Add more broth as necessary.
6. Stir in chard and simmer another 5 minutes until wilted. Season with salt and pepper.

Poultry Bacon Egg Sandwich

Ingredients:

- 8 lowfat turkey bacon rashers

- A pinch of dried dill and

- 2 eggs

- 2 oat bran galettes, flavored with your favorite herbs

- Black pepper, freshly ground.

Directions:

1. While preheating your grill to 356 degrees F, prepare 2 oat bran gazettes using the first Directions: but add more flavor by using fresh or dried herbs on the batter prior to cooking.
2. Once the gazettes are done, place each on a plate to set aside.

3. Use tin foil to line a baking tray on which you'll place the turkey bacon rashers for grilling. Put the baking tray under the grill to cook for 10 to 15 minutes.
4. When the bacon rashers are near cooked, start to poach the eggs either manually using the swirl method or us a Poach pod, a.k.a. a silicone egg poacher. Sprinkle each egg with a pinch of dried dill prior to poaching.
5. Once the bacons are done, place them on top of the oat bran gazettes, topped by a poached egg each. Use freshly ground black pepper to season and enjoy!

Oat Bran Muffins

Ingredients:

- ¼ cup skimmed milk

- 3 eggs

- 6 tablespoons fat free natural yogurt and

- 1 ½ cups oat bran

- 1 cup baking Splenda

- 1 teaspoon baking powder

- Vanilla extract, to taste.

Directions:

1. After mixing all the Ingredients: well, let them sit for about 20 minutes. While waiting, spray some cooking oil to line a nonstick muffin tin.

2. Fill the tin/s with the mixture and bake at 350 degrees F until done.

Cheesy Chivey Eggs Attack

Ingredients:

- 1 tablespoon fat free cream cheese
- 2 egg whites
- 1 tablespoon chives
- 1 whole egg

Directions:

1. In a large bowl, combine all the Ingredients: and scramble over medium heat with a bit of cooking spray on the pan or skillet to prevent sticking.

Shrimp Skewers With Lemon And Parsley

Ingredients:

- Grated zest of 1 lemon

- Finely chopped fresh parsley

- Salt and pepper (to taste)

- 810 fresh shrimps

- Lemon juice

- Extra virgin olive oil

- Skewers made of wood or metal.

Directions:

1. Prepare the shrimp: Clean the shrimp, removing the carapace and the back vein. You

can leave the tail on if you want a more decorative look.
2. Marinade: In a bowl, mix the lemon juice, the grated lemon zest, the chopped parsley, salt, pepper and a drizzle of extra virgin olive oil. Stir well to mix the Ingredients:.
3. Shrimp Marinade: Add the shrimp to the bowl with the marinade and make sure they are well coated in the dressing. Let it marinate for at least 1520 minutes to allow the flavors to develop.
4. Prepare the skewers: Thread the marinated shrimp onto the wooden or metal skewers, being careful not to overload the skewers.
5. Grilling the kebabs: Preheat a grill or nonstick skillet. Brush the skewers with a little extra virgin olive oil to prevent them from sticking to the cooking surface.

6. Cook the shrimp skewers for about 2 to 3 minutes per side, until cooked through and lightly browned.
7. Garnish and service: Arrange the shrimp skewers on a serving plate.
8. You can garnish them with some chopped fresh parsley and a squeeze of additional lemon juice, if you like. Serve them immediately as a tasty and light appetizer.
9. You can accompany the shrimp skewers with a fresh sauce, such as a lemon yogurt sauce, to add extra flavor. Make sure you don't overcook the shrimp to prevent them from becoming rubbery.

Chicken Salad With Celery And Mustard

Ingredients:

- 2 tablespoons light mayonnaise or Greek yogurt
- 1 tablespoon of Dijon mustard
- Juice of 1/2 lemon
- Salt and pepper (to taste)
- 200g of cooked and diced chicken breast
- 2 stalks of celery, cut into thin slices
- 1 spring onion, thinly sliced
- Chopped fresh parsley (optional, for garnish).

Directions:

1. Prepare the Ingredients: Sew up the chicken breast and cut it into evenly sized cubes. Cut the celery into thin slices and slice the spring onion.
2. Make the sauce: In a bowl, mix the light mayonnaise or Greek yogurt with the Dijon mustard. Add the lemon juice and mix well. Taste the sauce and adjust the salt and pepper to taste.
3. Assemble the Salad: In a large bowl, combine the diced chicken, sliced celery, and spring onion. Pour the prepared sauce over the Ingredients: and stir gently until all Ingredients: are well seasoned.
4. Adjust the Texture: If you want a creamier chicken salad, add some additional mayonnaise or Greek yogurt. If you prefer a lighter texture, you can add a little more lemon juice.

5. Garnish and Service: Transfer the Chicken Celery and Mustard Salad to a serving platter. If you like, you can garnish with some chopped fresh parsley for a touch of color and freshness. Serve the salad as an appetizer or as a light main course.
6. You can further customize the chicken salad by adding other Ingredients: like chopped nuts, raisins, or diced apples to vary the flavor and texture. Make sure the chicken is cooked through before using it in the salad.

Tofu Cubes Marinated In Spices

Ingredients:

- 1 teaspoon of sesame oil
- 1 teaspoon garlic powder
- 1 teaspoon of sweet paprika
- 1/2 teaspoon ground cumin
- 1/2 teaspoon ground black pepper
- 200g of ferrous tofu, cut into cubes
- 2 tablespoons low sodium soy sauce
- 1 tablespoon of apple cider vinegar or lemon juice
- Salt (optional, to taste)

- Chopped fresh parsley or cilantro for garnish (optional).

Directions:

1. Prepare the Ingredients: Cut the ferrous tofu into evenly sized cubes.
2. Prepare the marinade: In a bowl, combine the soy sauce, apple cider vinegar or lemon juice, sesame oil, garlic powder, sweet paprika, cumin powder, and black pepper. You can add a pinch of salt if you like, but be aware that the soy sauce is already salty.
3. Tofu Marinade: Add the tofu cubes to the marinade and stir gently to make sure they are well coated in the spice mixture.
4. Let it marinate for at least 30 minutes to allow the tofu to absorb the flavors. Cooking Tofu Cubes: Heat a nonstick skillet over medium high heat.
5. Add the marinated tofu cubes to the skillet and cook them for about 5 to 7 minutes,

turning them gently occasionally, until golden brown and crispy on all sides.

6. Garnish and Service: Transfer the spiced marinated tofu cubes to a serving platter. You can garnish with some chopped fresh parsley or cilantro for added freshness and color. Serve the tofu cubes as an appetizer or as a component of a light main course.
7. You can accompany the tofu cubes with a yogurt based sauce or soy sauce if you like. Experiment with the spices and customize the marinade to suit your tastes.

Egg And Onion Burin

Ingredients:

- ¾ tsp curry powder

- ¾ tsp turmeric

- 3 tsp tomato puree

- 3 tbsp rapeseed oil

- 6 eggs

- 2 onions, diced

- 3 tbsp fat free milk

- 3 cloves of garlic, crushed

- 3 green chilies, finely diced

- Cilantro, to garnish

Directions:

1. In a bowl, beat the eggs and milk together.
2. In a pan, use rapeseed oil to fry the onion, chilies and garlic till the onions become soft and pink.
3. Add the curry powder, turmeric and tomato puree to this and cook for 23 minutes more.
4. Next, add the egg mixture and stir till the eggs are cooked properly.
5. Garnish with chopped cilantro.

Chocolate Oat Bran Cereal

Ingredients:

- 12 tbsp oat bran

- 6 tsp cocoa powder (Make sure this is reduced fat and has no sugar added)

- Sweetener, according to taste

- 2 eggs

- 2 egg yolks

- Zero fat yogurt, to taste

Directions:

1. Preheat oven at 375 °F.
   In a bowl, mix the oat bran and cocoa powder together – make sure they are thoroughly mixed.
2. In another bowl, beat the eggs together – add the sweetener to this.
3. Add the egg mixture to the oat bran mixture and mix well.
4. Make small balls by rolling the resultant mixture, and place them on baking paper that has been placed on a baking sheet.
5. Press down on each ball using a fork.
6. Let this bake in the preheated oven for around 15 minutes.

7. Place it on a wire tray to let it cool.
8. Serve along with fat free yogurt, or crumble the cereal into the yogurt.

Breakfast Frittata

Ingredients:

- 1 ½ cups mushrooms, thinly sliced

- ¾ onion, diced

- 3 tbsp fresh chives, chopped

- Sea salt, according to taste

- 9 eggs

- 3 tbsp vegetable stock

- 1 ½ tomatoes, diced and deseeded

- Black pepper, ground, according to taste

Directions:

1. Use ½ tbsp of the stock to sauté the onion on medium heat, till the onion becomes soft.

2. Next, add another ½ tbsp of the stock, and add the mushrooms to it. Cook again for around 34 minutes, till fully cooked.
3. Add the rest of the stock, and the tomato and cook some more.
4. In a bowl, beat the eggs together. Next, add the chives and make sure the eggs are well seasoned.
5. Pour the egg mixture on the pan – cook on low heat.
6. Cover and continue to cook till the eggs become firm.
7. Cut into pieces according to a chosen size then serve.

Marinated Chicken Bites With Lemon Juice And Spices

Ingredients:

- Juice of 1 lemon
- Spices of your choice (such as paprika, pepper,
- Oregano, garlic powder)
- 2 chicken breasts cut into bite size pieces
- Salt (optional)

Directions:

1. In a bowl, mix the lemon juice with your chosen spices.
2. Add the chicken nuggets to the marinade and mix well to distribute the marinade evenly.

3. Cover the bowl with plastic wrap and leave the chicken to marinate in the refrigerator for at least 30 minutes.
4. Preheat a nonstick pan. Cook the marinated chicken nuggets on the skillet for about 8 to 10 minutes, turning occasionally, until browned and cooked through.
5. Add salt to taste, if desired. Serve the marinated chicken nuggets as an appetizer.

Tuna Carpaccio With Olive Oil Olive Oil And Balsamic Vinegar

Ingredients:

- Extra virgin olive oil
- Balsamic vinegar
- 200 g fresh thin tuna fillet
- Salt and pepper (optional)

Directions:

1. Arrange the tuna slices on a serving platter. Drizzle the tuna with a drizzle of extra virgin olive oil.
2. Drizzle a few drops of balsamic vinegar over the tuna. Add salt and pepper to taste, if desired.

3. Let the tuna Carpaccio stand for a few minutes to let the Ingredients: season. Serve the seasoned tuna Carpaccio as an appetizer.

Egg And Tomato Muffins

Ingredients:

- ½ onion
- Handful of parsley
- 1 green pepper
- 2 eggs
- ½ tsp. garlic powder
- 1 small tomato

Directions:

1. Preheat oven to 350°F. Combine Ingredients: with hand mixer or blender.
2. Place mixture in nonstick cupcake tray. Cook for 15 minutes. Tastes great topped with fat

free cream cheese!

Smooth And Creamy Cauliflower Mash

Ingredients:

- 3 tbsp. fat free cream cheese
- 12 garlic cloves, peeled
- 1 whole cauliflower
- Butter flavoring (optional)
- Salt and pepper to taste

Directions:

1. Break the cauliflower into pieces using hands. Place pieces in steamer with garlic cloves.
2. Steam until vegetables very tender (3035 minutes).
3. Using a piece of cheesecloth, squeeze as much moisture from the cauliflower as you can.

4. The drier you can get it, the better. Whip the cauliflower, garlic, cream cheese, butter flavoring, salt and pepper until smooth.
5. Serve similarly to a mashed potato.

Warm Roasted Red Pepper And Cauliflower Pate

Ingredients:

- 1 tsp. cumin

- ¼ roasted red pepper

- 1 garlic clove

- 1 whole cauliflower

- ½ c. skim milk

Directions:

1. Boil cauliflower in saucepan with water for 25 min. Drain well. Pour all the Ingredients: into a blender and blitz until well combined.

2. Pour the milk slowly into the blender until desired consistency is reached. Serve warm.

Green Smoothie

Ingredients:

- 1 banana

- ½ Cup cauliflower

- 2 dates

- 1 avocado

- 1 cup spinach

- 1 cup almond milk

Directions:

1. In a blender place all Ingredients: and blend until smooth
2. Pour smoothie in a glass and serve

Classic Strawberry Smoothie

Ingredients:

- 1 cup greek yogurt

- 1 cup orange juice

- 1 cup strawberries

- 1 banana

Directions:

1. In a blender place all Ingredients: and blend until smooth
2. Pour smoothie in a glass and serve

    -

Gobi Burr Muffins

Ingredients:

- Tbs ff plain yoghurt

- 1 tsp baking powder

- 2 whisked egg whites (dr oetker dried egg whites are good)

- 2 tsp splenda

- 1tbs wheatbran

- 2 tbs goji berries

- Cinnamon to taste

Directions:

1. Mix ingredients: together and stir in whisked egg whites (with a metal spoon)

2. Place in muffin moulds and bake for 16 mins at 180c. It will make about 4/5 muffins

Crockpot Flank Steak

Ingredients:

- 1 teaspoon of ginger,

- 1 tablespoon of sugar,

- 1 tablespoon of olive oil,

- 2 crushed cloves of garlic,

- 1 pound of flank steak,

- ¼ cup of soy sauce,

- 1 cup of pineapple chunks in their own juice (drain the liquid from the pineapples and save),

- 3 tablespoons of cornstarch, and

- 3 tablespoons of water.

Directions:

1. To prepare this slow cooker recipe for flank steak you will need to cut the flank steak into about 1/8 inch slices and put them into the slow cooker.
2. Next, mix soy sauce, pineapple juice, ginger, sugar, oil, and garlic in a bowl. Pour this mixture over the steak. Now, cover the slow cooker and cook on low for 6 hours. Turn the cooker
3. On high after the 6 hours and pour in the pineapple and then stir. Mix together the cornstarch and water in a bowl and add to the slow cooker. Cook on high and stir until the sauce
4. Begins to thicken. Most people enjoy this recipe over rice.
5. Cook on medium for around 6 to 8 hours. You can also add your own spices like salt, pepper, garlic salt, or onion powder.

Loaf Of Bread

Ingredients:

- 1 tspn baking powder

- 1 tspn salt

- 2 pkts quick fast yeast (8g per packet)

- 1 tbspn no fat plain yoghurt

- 4 tbspn fromage frais or philidelphia extra light cheese

- 3 eggs

- 8 tbspn oat bran

- 8 tbspn wheat bran

- 4 tbspn wheat germ

- 10 tbspn skim milk powder

- 4 or 5 tbspn warm water

Directions:

1. Use 2 bowls. In the first bowl mix the yeast, water and philidelphia cream cheese and give a good whisk.
2. Mix all the other ingredients together in a larger bowl.
3. Add the yeast mixture to the other ingredients and whisk well.
4. Pour mixture into a loaf tin (i line mine with baking paper) and cook in a hot oven 400 f for 10 minutes. Reduce temperature to 350 f degrees and cook for a further 20 minutes.

Pumpkin Soup

Ingredients:

- 1 apple, peeled, cored and chopped

- 1 stock, cube chicken flavour and low fat

- 1 tablespoon curry powder

- 115 g fromage frais, nonfat

- 1/4 pumpkin, peeled and cut into large pieces

- 1 onion, large

- Salt and pepper, to taste

Directions:

1. Put the pumpkin, onion, apple and bullion cube in a large saucepan, cover with water and cook for 20 30 minutes until soft.

2. After cooking, pureed the soup but make sure it is not made too smooth, so that you can still taste some bits of pumpkin melt in your mouth.
3. Add salt, pepper, curry powder and mix in the fromage frais or quark.

Creamy Surimi Salad

Ingredients:

- 1 tsp. Worcestershire sauce

- Zest of half a lemon + 1 tsp. Freshly squeezed lemon juice

- 1/4 tsp. Mustard powder

- 1/4 tsp. Garlic powder

- 1/4 tsp. Hot chili pepper sauce

- 100g surimi, thawed and cold (cut into bitesize chunks)

- 185g can tuna in brine or springwater (drained, and flaked finely)

- 3 tbs. Lowfat plain yogurt (less than 2%)

- Pepper (optional)

Directions:

1. Mix cold Surimi and tuna together well in bowl and set aside.
2. Mix all ingredients for sauce until combined evenly then add to Surimi and Tuna and mix well until the whole mixture is evenly covered in creamy mixture. Season with pepper and serve immediately.

Barbequed Cod On Wilted Spinach

Ingredients:

- 14 oz. cod steak fillets

- 1 bag of washed baby spinach leaves juice of ½ lemon salt and pepper to taste paprika to taste

Directions:

1. On a barbeque (or grill pan on the stove), cook the fish for about 20 minutes or until all the flesh has turned white.
2. While the fish is grilling, in a large nonstick frying pan, heat the juice of the ½ lemon, add the baby spinach and steam cook this for a few moments until the leaves begin to soften.
3. Remove from heat and place on a serving plate.

4. Season with salt and pepper. Pour the lemon juice over the top, and sprinkle with paprika. Lay fish over the top of the spinach, and serve immediately.

The Ideal Cookie "One" According To Dukan

Ingredients:

- 2 yolks have eggs

- Sugarzamliquid milford1 cap

- A pinch of salt

- 40 ml. Cold water

- 1 tbsp protein isolate15gri have soy isolate

- 1 tbsp cornstarch20 gr(1 extra) + a little for molding if needed

- 1 tbsp wheat gluten20 gr

- 1 heaping tbsp skimmed milk powder som   30 gr   (1 extra)

- 1 tsp baking powder

- 1 tbsp any vegetable oil15 grnorm for 1 day

- Tastearomatics, lemon zest or juice, vanillin, nuts, goji berries, etc.

- Sprinkle as desiredpoppy, sesame, flax seeds, chia, etc.

Directions:

1. The directions: is very simple, the result is great!
2. Mix all dry ingredients:
3. Sifting them
4. Separately, beat the yolks + water + sugar + butter
5. Mix everything together until smooth
6. Put the dough in the refrigerator for 3040 minutes
7. The finished dough (after the refrigerator) should be viscous and thick
8. We sprinkle a little with starch or isolate.

9. If suddenly the dough turned out to be watery, this may be due to the quality of the som, do not worry! Do not add anything else, put it immediately on a baking sheet with a wet spoon or pastry bag
10. We form a sausage from the dough, cut into equal parts cookie blanks
11. Put on a baking sheet, form cookies.
12. Keep in mind, it rises almost twice. Therefore, if you want a more "sandy" version of cookies, make it thinner.
13. Bake at 180°c without convection for 15 minutes (depending on size)
14. Do not overdry! The cookies will dry out a little while cooling.

Crunchy Biscuits "Simple" According To Dukan

Ingredients:

- 1 tsp baking powder

- 2 eggs

- 1 tbsp any vegetable oil15 gr

- Sucrose

- A pinch of salt

- 2 tbsp oat bran30 granny grinding

- 2 tbsp protein isolate30 grid have soy isolate

- 12 tbsp cornstarch20 gr(1 extra)

- Tastearomatics

- Additiveslemon zest or juice, vanillin, nuts, goji berries, etc.

- sprinkle on requestpoppy, sesame, flax seeds, chia, etc. I have sunflower seed

Directions:

1. The directions: of these cookies according to dukan is simply elementary! Even a novice hostess will cope =)
2. To begin with, pour all the dry ingredients: into a bowl, mix
3. Add eggs, butter, sweetener. If you use additives add now too
4. Beat with a mixer until smooth.
5. Leave the dough to swell for 10 minutes.
6. In this directions:, you can use bran of any grinding! It won't affect the taste. I used coarse bran here.
7. The finished dough is quite thick. The approximate consistency is a little thicker than

on pancakes. The dough should spread a little, but keep its shape.
8. If you have a liquid dough, add wheat bran or more isolate to the required density.
9. Now we shift the dough into a pastry bag or a regular tight bag (we just cut off the corner of the bag)
10. Place small cookies on a baking sheet. They expand quite a bit when baked.
11. I decided to sprinkle the cookies with sunflower seeds.
12. You can use whatever topping you like, or don't use it at all.
13. Preheat the oven to 180 c
14. Bake cookies for 20-25 minutes (depending on size) until desired "dryness" without convection
15. Keep in mind they will harden a bit as they cool.
16. The finished cookies are very tasty and crispy!

17. This biscuit according to dukan is stored very well. You can take it on the road!
18. It is better to store in a paper bag so that the cookies do not "suffocate"

Khachaturian With A Boat In A Frying Pan According To Dukan

Ingredients:

- 180 gr cottage cheese better from a pack, not grainy!
- 1 tsp baking powder10 gr
- 1 tsp frying oils of necessity
- 3 tbsp oat bran45 gr
- 1 egg not very big
- 30 gr fat free cheese up to 7% fat(1 extra)
- Salt

Directions:

1. The directions: is very simple and takes very little time!
2. To begin with, the egg is divided into protein and yolk. Leave the yolk for the filling.
3. Mix protein with bran and leave to swell
4. Add cottage cheese, baking powder and salt to the bran
5. Mix until smooth. The dough is quite dense
6. In a frying pan with wet hands, we form boats with a recess in the center.
7. If you form two khachapuri, then you will need one more yolk for the filling.
8. Fry khachapuri (recessed down) in a teaspoon of oil under a lid over low heat.
9. We turn over. Put the yolk(s) in the recess. We try to keep it whole and not spread
10. Sprinkle with grated cheese. Fry until cooked on a very low heat under the lid

11. Important! If you didn't find cheese with a fat content of less than 7%, but you really want khachapuri, you can take cheese a little fatter, but less than a gram, you should fit into 2 dips
12. We look at the fat content of cheese not in dry matter, but in bju.
13. We calculate cheese according to the formula 210 / fat content of cheese \u003d gr \u003d 1 dop
14. Let's look at an example. The fat content of cheese according to bju is 12%. We calculate according to the formula 210/12 \u003d 17.5 gr. It turns out 17.5 g of cheese with a fat content of 12% \u003d 1 dop. So in this directions: you can use 35 grams of cheese using a fat content of 12%, this will be 2 dop
15. Ready! Khachapuri is delicious both hot and cold!

Thai Chicken With Broccoli And Shirataki Noodles

Ingredients:

- 1 teaspoon powdered stevia extract such as Dukan Diet Organic Stevia

- 1 tablespoon red wine vinegar

- ¼ cup fresh lime juice

- Salt

- 1 tablespoon cornstarch

- 2 (7ounce) packages of shirataki noodles, such as Dukan Diet Shirataki Noodles, prepared according to the Directions:.

- 1 tablespoon finely chopped fresh cilantro

- ¼ teaspoon vegetable oil

- 4 boneless, skinless chicken breasts, chopped into ½inch cubes

- 1 egg plus 2 egg whites, lightly beaten

- 2 scallions, thinly sliced

- 1 head of broccoli, chopped into small florets

- 3 garlic cloves, chopped

- Lowsodium soy sauce

- Thai hot sauce, such as Sriracha (optional)

Directions:

1. Heat a large nonstick skillet over medium heat. Add ⅛ teaspoon of the oil and wipe out any excess with a paper towel. Add the chicken, and cook thoroughly, stirring often, about 5 minutes.

2. Add the eggs and cook, stirring often, for an additional 3 minutes. Transfer to a dish and set aside.
3. Return the skillet to a burner and adjust the heat to low. Add the remaining oil and wipe out any excess with a paper towel.
4. Add the scallions and cook, stirring often, until soft, about 5 minutes.
5. Add the broccoli and 2 tablespoons of water. Cover the skillet and cook for 5 minutes. Add the garlic, stevia, vinegar, lime juice, chicken, and salt to taste. Stir until combined. In a small bowl, thoroughly combine the cornstarch and 1 tablespoon of water.
6. Pour the cornstarch mixture over the broccoli and chicken, and stir it in very quickly and vigorously so that none of it sticks to the bottom of the skillet. Remove the pan from the heat.

7. To serve, divide the cooked noodles among 4 bowls and top with equal portions of the chicken mixture. Garnish with chopped cilantro, and add soy sauce and hot sauce to taste.

Shirataki Noodles With Balsamic Vinegar

Ingredients:

- 2 garlic cloves, finely chopped

- Salt and freshly ground black pepper

- 2 tomatoes, finely diced

- 1 red onion, finely chopped

- ¼ cup balsamic vinegar

- 2 tablespoons chopped fresh basil

- 2 (7ounce) packages of shirataki noodles, such as Dukan Diet Shirataki Noodles, prepared according to the Directions:.

Directions:

1. In a large bowl, thoroughly combine the vinegar, basil, and garlic. Add salt and pepper to taste.
2. Add the tomatoes and onion, stir well, cover, and leave at room temperature to marinate for 1 to 2 hours.
3. Add the prepared noodles to the tomato mixture, and season with salt and pepper to taste before serving.

Thousand Inland Dressing

Ingredients:

- 1 teaspoon yellow onion finely grated

- 1 1/2 tablespoons apple cider vinegar

- 23 tablespoons water

- 2 1/2 tablespoons pickle Relish (or sweet pickles)

- 1/2 cup firm tofu drained and not pressed (Silken or regular)

- 4 tablespoons ketchup

- 34 dashes Tabasco sauce (optional)

Directions:

1. If using regular tofu, use a small blender for smoothness and combine all ingredients except pickle relish and only 1 tablespoon of water.
2. Blend well. Also, you may want to start with 1 tablespoon of apple cider vinegar and taste before adding more. You may not need a blender for Silken tofu so in that case, whisk everything in a small bowl.
3. Add pickle relish and stir to combine. The relish may add liquid but if the dressing is too thick, add a few more tablespoons of water. Refrigerate in a covered container and chill for several hours to blend flavors. Can be stored up to a week.
4. Serve on salads, as a dressing for burgers or a Reuben sandwich.

Quinoa Salad With Cauliflower

Ingredients:

- 1 1/2 cups raw broccoli diced 1/4"

- 1/2 cup parsley diced

- Dressing

- 3 tablespoons lemon juice

- 3 tablespoons apple cider vinegar

- 2 tablespoon dijon mustard

- 2 teaspoon lowsodium tamari

- 1 cup quinoa rinsed

- 1 large carrot peeled and grated

- 1 medium bell red pepper seeded and diced 1/4"

- 1/3 medium red onion (about 1/2 cup)

- 1 1/2 cups nosalt chickpeas drained and rinsed

- 1 1/2 cups raw cauliflower diced 1/4"

- Freshly ground black pepper to taste

Directions:

1. Add rinsed quinoa and 2 cups water to a saucepan over mediumhigh heat. Heat to boiling, lower to a simmer, cover and cook for 15 minutes or until the water has evaporated. Add to a large bowl to cool why preparing the rest of the Ingredients:.

2. Once cooled add the carrot, bell pepper, red onion, chickpeas, cauliflower, broccoli, and parsley to the bowl with the quinoa and stir to combine.
3. Add the dressing ingredients to a small bowl and whisk. Pour 1/2 of the dressing over the salad and mix well. Taste and check to see if you want to use the whole recipe
4. Refrigerate leftovers in an airtight container for 34 days.

Baked Salmon Omelet

Ingredients:

- 2 tablespoons fat free natural yogurt

- 1 tablespoon dried dill

- 1 tablespoon fresh chives, chopped

- 6 whole eggs

- 200 grams smoked salmon

- Black pepper, freshly ground

Directions:

1. While preheating the oven to 356 degrees F, chop 2/3 of the smoked salmon roughly (for mixing with the eggs) and cut the remaining 1/3 into strips (for garnishing).

2. Mix the yogurt, eggs and dried dill in a bowl and when done, mix in the roughly chopped salmon well and season with freshly ground pepper. Transfer this mixture into a silicone cake tin mold or loaf pan, arrange the remaining 1/3 salmon on top of the omelet and shower with chopped chives.
3. Bake in the middle shelf of the preheated oven for 40 minutes. Remove from oven, allow to cool and enjoy!

Caraway Chops

Ingredients:

- 1 tablespoon caraway seeds

- 2 pork chops and

- 1 lemon

- Salt and pepper.

Directions:

1. While heating up the oven to 356 degrees F, remove all visible fat from the pork chops and put on a plate. Set aside.
2. Powder the caraway seeds using a pestle and mortar. Rub the powdered seeds all over the lean pork chops and season further with salt and pepper.
3. On a heated nonstick pan over medium heat, sear the chops and when they start to brown,

transfer them to a roasting tin in the heated oven until cooked through.
4. Enjoy by squeezing lemon juice over the chops.

Curettes And Fresh Cheese Omelets

Ingredients:

- 50g of diced fresh cheese (such as mozzarella or ricotta)

- Fresh parsley, chopped

- Salt and pepper (to taste)

- 2 medium curettes, cut into thin rounds

- 4 eggs

- Extra virgin olive oil (for cooking).

Directions:

1. Prepare the curettes: Cut the curettes into thin slices. You can also grate them if you prefer a finer texture.

2. Beat Eggs: In a bowl, beat the eggs with a fork until smooth. Add the chopped fresh parsley, salt and pepper. Mix well.
3. Add the Curettes: Add the chopped courgettes to the beaten eggs. Make sure the courgettes is evenly distributed in the mixture.
4. Add the Cream Cheese: Add the cubes of cream cheese to the egg and courgettes mixture. You can also stir lightly to distribute the cheese evenly.
5. Cooking the omelette: Heat a little extra virgin olive oil in a nonstick pan over mediumhigh heat. Pour the egg, courgettes, and cheese mixture into the skillet. Level the mixture with a spoon or spatula to spread it evenly across the pan.
6. Cook over mediumlow heat: Cover the pan with a lid and cook the omelet over mediumlow heat for about 810 minutes, until

cooked through the bottom and the eggs are set.
7. Cooking over high heat: Remove the lid and cook the frittata over high heat for about 23 minutes, until the top is lightly browned.
8. Service: Transfer the omelet to a serving plate and cut it into wedges or squares. You can garnish with some chopped fresh parsley. Serve the courgettes and fresh cheese omelette as an appetizer or as a light main course, accompanied by a fresh salad or grilled vegetables.
9. Courgettes and cottage cheese omelette is a delicious and healthy option for the Dukan diet. You can customize the recipe by adding other vegetables, such as cherry tomatoes or peppers, according to your tastes. Be sure to cook the omelette over mediumlow heat to ensure even cooking.

Salmon Rolls With Asparagus

Ingredients:

- 810 fresh asparagus

- Lemon juice

- Extra virgin olive oil

- 4 slices of smoked salmon

- Salt and pepper (to taste).

Directions:

1. Prepare the asparagus: Wash them and cut the woody parts at the base of the asparagus. You can also lightly peel the undersides of the asparagus to make them more tender.
2. Cook the asparagus: Bring a pot of salted water to a boil and cook the asparagus for

about 3 to 4 minutes, until tender but still crunchy.
3. Drain and immediately immerse them in cold water to stop the cooking. Drain them again and dry them gently.
4. Prepare the Salmon: Spread the smoked salmon slices out on a clean work surface. Brush them lightly with lemon juice to add a touch of freshness.
5. Assemble the rolls: Take a slice of smoked salmon and place 23 cooked asparagus at the base of the slice.
6. Gently roll the salmon around the asparagus, forming a tight wrap. Repeat the process with the other salmon slices and the remaining asparagus.
7. Dressing: Brush the salmon rolls with a drizzle of extra virgin olive oil. Add salt and pepper to taste.

8. Service: You can serve the salmon rolls with asparagus as an appetizer or as a light main course. You can accompany it with a light lemon sauce or with a fresh salad.
9. Salmon rolls with asparagus are an elegant and flavorful option for the Dukan diet. The smoked salmon offers a rich taste, while the asparagus adds freshness and crunch. You can customize the recipe by adding herbs like dill or parsley to enhance the flavor.

Greek Chicken Salad With Cucumbers And Olives

Ingredients:

- 1/2 red onion, thinly sliced

- 50g of black olives, pitted and sliced

- 50g feta cheese, crumbled

- Lemon juice

- Extra virgin olive oil

- 200g chicken breast, cooked and diced

- 1 cucumber, diced

- 1 tomato, diced

- dried oregano

- Salt and pepper (to taste).

Directions:

1. Prepare the Chicken Breast: Cook the chicken breast in steam or in salted water until fully cooked. Let it cool, then cut it into cubes.
2. Prepare the Ingredients: Cut the cucumber into cubes, the tomato into cubes, the red onion into thin slices and the black olives into slices. Crumble the feta cheese.
3. Assemble the Salad: In a large bowl, combine the chicken, cucumber, tomato, onion, olives, and feta cheese. Stir gently to combine Ingredients:.
4. Dressing: Squeeze a little lemon juice over the salad and add a drizzle of extra virgin olive oil. Sprinkle with dried oregano. Add salt and pepper to taste. Toss the salad well to distribute the dressing evenly.

5. Resting: Let the salad rest in the refrigerator for at least 30 minutes to allow the flavors to meld.
6. Service: Transfer the Greek Chicken Salad to a platter. You can garnish with a few slices of lemon and fresh parsley leaves. Serve the salad as an appetizer or as a light main course.
7. Greek Chicken Salad with Cucumbers and Olives is a tasty and healthy option for the Dukan diet.
8. The combination of fresh and flavorful Ingredients: offers a dish full of proteins and nutrients. You can customize the recipe by adding other typical Greek Ingredients:, such as peppers or fresh oregano.

Mediterranean Chicken Drumsticks

Ingredients:

- 3 tbsp mustard

- 1 tbsp fresh rosemary

- 1 tbsp fresh thyme

- 1 lb. chicken drumsticks, skinless

- ½ tbsp black peppercorns

- Salt, according to taste

Directions:

1. Using a knife, make two 5inch slits on each side of each drumstick.
2. In a food processor, blend the peppercorns, mustard, rosemary, thyme and salt. Use water to make the marinade thinner, as necessary.

3. Coat the drumsticks in the marinade and cover the bowl using cling wrap. Refrigerate for 34 hours.
4. Preheat the broiler (at medium).
5. Arrange the drumsticks on a baking sheet and broil for 45 minutes. Then, use tongs to flip them and broil again, for a similar duration.
6. Tent using foil for 20 minutes.

Chicken Caesar Salad

Ingredients:

- Grated parmesan cheese
- 2 tablespoons light mayonnaise
- Lemon juice
- Chopped anchovy fillets (optional)
- 2 grilled chicken breasts, cut into slices
- Romaine salad mix or lettuce
- Toasted bread croutons
- Salt and pepper to taste.

Directions:

1. In a bowl, mix light mayonnaise with lemon juice, chopped anchovy fillets (if desired), salt, and pepper to create Caesar dressing.
2. Arrange the salad mix on a serving platter. Add the grilled chicken slices on top of the salad. Season with Caesar dressing and toss well.
3. Add the toasted bread croutons and grated parmesan cheese on top of the salad. Serve the chicken Caesar salad as an appetizer.

Bristol With Arugula And Parmesan Shavings

Ingredients:

- 30 g of Parmesan shavings

- Extra virgin olive oil

- 100 g bresaola, 50 g arugula

- Lemon juice

Directions:

1. Arrange the bresaola on a serving plate. Season the arugula with a little olive oil and lemon juice, then place it on top of the bresaola.
2. Sprinkle Parmesan shavings over the bresaola and arugula. If you wish, you can add some freshly ground black pepper to give additional flavor. Serve and enjoy!

Spinach Cudgel

Ingredients:

- ¾ c. egg whites

- 1 bag Shirataki noodles

- ½ c. baby Spinach

- ½ red bell pepper

- Spray cooking oil

Directions:

1. Rinse Shirataki noodles in hot water. Drain. Place on noodles on paper towels to dry. Set aside.
2. Spray a medium size non stick fry pan with cooking oil, and set on medium heat.
3. Add egg whites, noodles, spinach and pepper to the pan.

4. After about 15 minutes or so, check use a spatula to see what the cudgel looks like.
5. If it is golden on the bottom and set on top, flip cudgel over and allow to pan fry for another 15 minutes or so until both sides are golden brown.

Tender Grilled Venison

Ingredients:

- 1 onions, sliced
- 10 oz venison steak
- Salt and pepper to taste
- 1 c. fat free yogurt
- 1 carrot, chopped
- ½ tsp. garlic salt
- Spray cooking oil

Directions:

1. Marinate steak overnight (at least 8 hours) in yogurt, onion, 1 diced carrot and garlic salt.
2. Remove meat from marinade and rinse under cold water. Season with salt pepper.

3. Spray grill with a few sprays of cooking oil. Allow to heat until smoking.
4. Cook venison until desired wellness is reached. Allow steak to rest, covered for 5 minutes.

Spaghetti With Beef Broth

Ingredients:

- ½ c. fresh tomatoes, diced
- ⅓ c. beef stock
- 34 tbsp. powdered beef gelatin
- Spaghetti or Italian seasoning
- 1 8 oz package Shirataki noodles
- 6 cherry tomatoes, halved
- ½ lb ground beef, cooked and drained
- ½ c. onion, diced
- 1 clove garlic, diced
- 3 celery stalks, just the tops

- 1 can tomatoes

- Handful of chives, chopped

- Cooking oil spray

Directions:

1. Sauté onions and garlic in a deep, nonstick fry pan with a bit of spray cooking oil.
2. Add can of tomatoes, celery tops, and fresh tomato. Then, add spaghetti spice, beef broth and gelatin (or cornstarch).
3. As this comes to a boil, rinse and dry fry noodles in a skillet for a few minutes. Add noodles to sauce and simmer for 15 minutes.
4. Add fresh cherry tomato halves and simmer for another 15 minutes, stirring occasionally.
5. After plating, sprinkle with fat free Parmesan cheese and chopped chives. Tastes great with salad topped with creamy dressing.

Chicken With Lemon And Capers

Ingredients:

- 800g (1lb 12oz) chicken breasts, cut into thin slices
- Grated zest of 1 lemon
- 1 tbsp small capers, drained and rinsed
- 75ml (2½ fl oz) lemon juice
- 5 basil leaves, finely chopped
- 3 drops of oil
- 1 red onion, finely chopped
- Salt and black pepper

Directions:

1. In a nonstick frying pan (oiled and wiped with kitchen paper), panfry the onion until it turns goldenbrown, then put to one side.
2. Brown the chicken slices in the same pan over a medium heat. Add the onion, lemon zest, capers, lemon juice, basil, salt and black pepper. Serve piping hot.

Cod With Mustard Sauce

Ingredients:

- 150g (5½ oz) fatfree natural yoghurt

- 1 tbsp mustard

- Lemon juice (to taste)

- 2 tbsp capers

- 1 cod fillet

- Salt and black pepper

- 1 bunch of parsley, finely chopped

Directions:

1. Sprinkle some salt over the cod fillet and steam for 8–10 minutes (depending on its thickness).

2. In the meantime, put the yoghurt, mustard, some lemon juice, capers, parsley and black pepper into a saucepan.
3. Warm over a gentle heat and pour over the cooked fish.

Vietnamese Beef

Ingredients:

- 1 large piece of ginger, grated

- Black pepper

- 3 drops of oil

- 4 garlic cloves, crushed

- 400g (14oz) sirloin steak

- 2 tbsp soy sauce

- 1 tbsp oyster sauce

- A few coriander leaves, chopped Cut the beef into 1cm (about ½ in) cubes.

Directions:

1. Mix with the soy sauce, oyster sauce, ginger and black pepper, and leave to marinate for 30 minutes.
2. Then cook with the garlic over a high heat for 1015 seconds, stirring quickly.
3. Garnish with coriander leaves.

Chicken Curry With Crunchy Vegetables

Ingredients:

- 1 curette, thinly sliced

- 2 tablespoons curry paste (to taste, depending on desired level of spiciness)

- 200ml of coconut milk

- Salt and pepper (to taste)

- Chopped fresh coriander (for garnish, optional)

- 200g chicken breast, cut into small pieces

- 1 tablespoon coconut oil or extra virgin olive oil

- 1 onion, thinly sliced

- 2 bell peppers (one red and one yellow), cut into strips

- 1 carrot, thinly sliced

- Lime juice (from half a lime, optional)

Directions:

1. Preparing the Vegetables: Heat the coconut oil or extra virgin olive oil in a nonstick skillet over medium high heat.
2. Add the onion, peppers, carrot and curettes. Cook the vegetables for about 5 to 7 minutes, stirring occasionally, until crisp but tender. Remove the vegetables from the pan and set them aside.
3. Directions: of the chicken: In the same pan, add the chicken pieces and cook them until they are browned and cooked through. Adjust the salt and pepper to your liking.

4. Adding the Curry: Reduce the heat to medium low and add the curry paste to the pan. Mix well to coat the chicken evenly.
5. Adding the Coconut Milk: Pour the coconut milk into the pan with the chicken and curry. Stir well to combine the Ingredients:. Simmer over medium low heat for about 5 to 7 minutes, until the chicken is tender and the curry has thickened slightly.
6. Composition of the dish: Take back the crunchy vegetables you had set aside and add them to the pan with the chicken and curry. Gently stir to incorporate the vegetables into the curry sauce.
7. Garnish: If you like, you can garnish the chicken curry with some freshly chopped coriander for an extra flavorful twist. You can also drizzle some lime juice over the dish for a fresh note.

8. Chicken Curry with Crispy Vegetables is a delicious and flavor some dish that is suitable for the Dukan diet. You can serve it alone or accompanied by a portion of brown basmati rice or steamed vegetables. Make sure you choose a curry paste that fits your spicy tolerance.

Garlic And Dill Chicken Breasts

Ingredients:

- 1 onion, finely diced
- 1 tsp rapeseed oil
- ½ tbsp lemon juice
- 1 tsp corn flour
- Salt, to taste
- 2 chicken breasts, skinless and boneless
- ½ cup chicken stock
- 2 cloves of garlic, minced
- 1 tbsp fresh dill, chopped
- Pepper, to taste

Directions:

1. Cook the chicken breast in a pan, for about 34 minutes on each side – till it becomes brown. In another pan, add some oil and then cook garlic and onion for 34 more minutes.
2. In a bowl, mix the chicken stock, dill, lemon juice and corn flour. Add this to the pan with the onion and stir till the corn flour mix becomes thick – add salt and pepper according to taste.
3. Add the chicken to this pan, and let it cook some more – for about 5 minutes.
4. Garnish with some more fresh dill.

Steak Au Pire

Ingredients:

- ½ onion, finely chopped

- 2 tbsp skimmed milk

- 4 tbsp zero fat from age frays

- ½ tbsp Dijon mustard

- 2 beef tenderloin steaks

- 1 tbsp black peppercorns, crushed

- Salt, to taste

Directions:

1. Season the steaks with salt, and let it stand for half an hour. Then, coat the steaks with black peppercorns.
2. In a pan, dry fry the steaks, till it is cooked to your liking.
3. Wrap the steaks with foil and set aside.
4. Next, fry the onion in a pan till it becomes soft. Simultaneously, in another pan, heat milk and add Dijon mustard to it.

5. Remove this from the heat and add milk and fromage frais. When they have combined completely, continue heating it.
6. Place the steak on plates, and pour this sauce over it.

Grilled Vegetable Skewers

Ingredients:

- Red onions
- Button mushrooms
- Extra virgin olive oil
- Zucchini
- Bell peppers
- Salt and pepper to taste.

Directions:

1. Cut zucchini, bell peppers, red onions, and button mushrooms into similar sized pieces.
2. Thread the cut Ingredients: onto skewers, alternating the different types of vegetables.

3. Brush the skewers with extra virgin olive oil and season with salt and pepper.
4. Heat a grill or nonstick skillet. Cook the grilled vegetable skewers for 4 to 6 minutes per side, until soft and lightly browned.
5. Serve the grilled vegetable skewers hot.

Guacamole With Celery Chips

Ingredients:

- 1 small onion, finely chopped

- Fresh cilantro, chopped (optional)

- Salt and pepper to taste

- Celery for the chips

- 2 ripe avocados

- Lemon juice

- 1 ripe tomato, diced

Directions:

1. In a bowl, mash the avocados with a fork until creamy. Add lemon juice to prevent the avocado from oxidizing.

2. Add the diced tomato, chopped onion, and fresh cilantro (if desired). Mix all Ingredients: well and season with salt and pepper to taste.
3. Cut the celery into sticks for the chips. Serve the guacamole with the celery chips.

Tofu And Veggie Stir Fry

Ingredients:

- 1 tsp. fresh ginger, grated
- Juice from 1 lemon
- 1 tsp. lemongrass, crushed
- 8 oz. firm tofu, cut into even sized pieces
- ½ c. broccoli florets
- 2 zucchini, sliced
- 1 garlic clove, finely chopped
- 1 tbsp. low sodium soy sauce

Directions:

1. Mix the garlic, ginger, lemongrass, lemon juice and soy sauce together in a bowl.

2. Add tofu to a nonstick frying pan on a high heat.
3. Stir often to prevent the tofu sticking.
4. Once the tofu is lightly browned, add vegetables and 2 tablespoons of water.
5. Stir contents of skillet for a few minutes until they are cooked, but still quite firm. Add soy sauce, and cook for another minute.

Chilled Seafood Salad

Ingredients:

- 23 garlic cloves, finely chopped or pressed

- 3 lemons

- Fresh parsley (to taste)

- 1 lb scallops

- 1 lb calamari, cut into bite size pieces

- 2 celery stalks, diced

- 1 lb shrimp, cleaned and deveined

Directions:

1. Set a large pot of water to boil. Cut up a half of lemon, and squeeze fresh juice into boiling water.

2. Also throw in juiced lemon. Boil shrimp for approximately 5 minutes (until pink). Remove with slotted spoon and set in an ice bath. When cool, cut into bite sized pieces.
3. Then, add calamari to boil. Cook for about 3 minutes (until opaque). Remove with slotted spoon and set aside to cool.
4. Add scallops to same pot. Cook for 5 minutes.
5. Set aside to cool. In a large container (with lid), place garlic, celery, juice of 2 lemons, cooled seafood, parsley, salt and pepper. Cover container and shake well. Refrigerate for at least 2 hours before serving.

Italian Sausage and Noodles in Cream Sauce

Ingredients:

- 2 oz fat free cream cheese

- 1 c. fat free milk

- Fresh parsley (to taste)

- 1 pack chicken sausage (spicy Italian), about 5 links

- Tofu Shirataki Noodles

Directions:

1. Remove the sausage from casing, and brown in a nonstick skillet over medium heat.
2. Once cooked, add milk and cream cheese.
3. Bring to a low boil and reduce heat. Prepare noodles according to package Directions:.
4. Add cooked noodles to sausage mixture. Cook a bit more until noodles well coated and sauce thickens. Garnish with parsley.

Cardamom Tart

Ingredients:

- 2 tablespoons lemon juice

- Pastry sheets

- 45 pears

Cardamom filling

- ¼ Lb. Flour

- 1 ¼ tsp cardamom

- 2 eggs

- ½ Lb. Butter

- ½ Lb. Brown sugar

- ½ Lb. Almonds

Directions:

1. Preheat oven to 400 F, unfold pastry sheets and place them on a baking sheet
2. Toss together all Ingredients: together and mix well
3. Spread mixture in a single layer on the pastry sheets
4. Before baking decorate with your desired fruits
5. Bake at 400 F for 2225 minutes or until golden brown
6. When ready remove from the oven and serve

Apple Tart

Ingredients:

- Pastry sheets

Filling

- 1 lb. Apples

- 150 ml double cream

- 2 eggs

- 1 tsp lemon juice

- 3 oz. Brown sugar

Directions:

1. Preheat oven to 400 F, unfold pastry sheets and place them on a baking sheet
2. Toss together all Ingredients: together and mix well
3. Spread mixture in a single layer on the pastry sheets
4. Before baking decorate with your desired fruits
5. Bake at 400 F for 2225 minutes or until golden brown
6. When ready remove from the oven and serve

Muesli Bars According To Dukan

Ingredients:

- 50 gr raw peanuts(according to the oil rate)
- 22 gr. Walnut(according to the oil rate)(for 1 day)
- Sucrose
- 4 tbsp oat bran60 gr
- 60 ml. Skimmed milk (liquid)(0.5%1.5%)
- 34 tbsp catfish (skimmed milk powder)60 gr
- 1 egg

For glaze

- 120 ml. Skimmed milk (liquid)(0.5%1.5%)

- 34 tbsp catfish (skimmed milk powder)60 gram Sucrose

- Aromatic "Chocolate" or "Cocoa Beans" (if any)

Directions:

1. Let's start cooking by chopping nuts.
2. The degree of grinding depends on your tastes. I love when the nuts are crushed not quite into powder, but large pieces are felt. You can do this with a coffee grinder, blender or rolling pin.
3. Fill the bran with milk. Leave to swell for 1015 minutes.
4. During this time, the bran will completely absorb the milk.
5. To the swollen bran, add chopped nuts, skimmed milk powder (som), sucrose
6. Adding an egg

7. The density of the dough depends, among other things, on the degree of crushing of the nuts and on the size of the egg. So that the dough does not turn out to be very liquid, i recommend putting the protein in the dough first, if it is very thick, add the yolk already.
8. Stir the dough until smooth. The mass should be thick enough and not spread.
9. We spread the mass on a silicone mat or parchment (only if you are sure of the quality of the parchment, and nothing will stick to it)
10. Level the mass with a spatula or a wide knife. The thickness of 0.50.7 mm is the most successful.
11. We outline future bars with a knife.
12. We bake at 160170c for 1015 minutes, depending on the thickness, until a light golden crust.
13. Remove from oven, turn upside down and bake for another 57 minutes.

14. Do not overdry! Keep in mind that after cooling they will still harden.
15. While the bars are baking, we make the frosting.
16. Pour dry milk into a cup, add sugar. And add liquid milk in a tablespoon.
17. We bring to the required density
18. Don't make the frosting runny or it won't set!
19. We take out the bars from the oven, cut them while still hot.
20. Place immediately on a wire rack and cover with frosting. You can do this with a culinary brush, or you can simply "bathe" the bars with one side in the glaze.
21. With the remaining glaze, cover the bars with a second layer.
22. Leave to cool for 10 minutes on the table, then put in the refrigerator until completely cooled.

23. The icing should cool completely and not be smeared.
24. Ready! They turn out very tasty. Fragrant and nutritious bars! Keep for a long time! But trust me, they won't last long.

Swordfish Carpaccio With Arugula And Lemon

Ingredients:

- Lemon juice
- Extra virgin olive oil
- Salt and pepper (to taste)
- 200g of fresh swordfish fillet
- fresh arugula
- Parmesan flakes (optional, for garnish).

Directions:

1. Prepare the swordfish: Make sure the swordfish fillet is fresh and free from skin and bones. Cut it into thin slices using a sharp knife.

2. Prepare the marinade: In a bowl, mix the lemon juice with the extra virgin olive oil. Add salt and pepper to taste and mix well to create a light marinade.
3. Swordfish marinade: Arrange the swordfish slices on a plate or pan and pour the prepared marinade over them. Make sure the slices are well covered in the marinade. Marinate in the refrigerator for at least 15-20 minutes to allow the fish to absorb the flavors.
4. Composition of the carpaccio: Take a serving dish and arrange the slices of marinated swordfish evenly. Cover the fish with a bed of fresh arugula.
5. Dressing: Drizzle a little fresh lemon juice and extra virgin olive oil on the carpaccio. Add salt and pepper to taste.
6. Garnish (optional): To add a touch of taste and decoration, you can sprinkle the carpaccio with a few flakes of Parmesan.

7. Service: Serve the swordfish carpaccio with arugula and lemon as an appetizer or as a light dish. You can accompany it with toasted wholemeal bread or crunchy crackers.
8. Swordfish carpaccio with arugula and lemon is a fresh and light option for the Dukan diet. Be sure to use fresh, high-quality swordfish for the best flavor and texture. You can adapt the recipe by adding other ingredients such as cherry tomatoes, capers or olives to enrich the taste. Remember to consume raw fish only if you are sure of its freshness and origin.

Chicken Meatballs With Tomato Sauce

Ingredients:

For the meatballs:

- 2 tablespoons of grated cheese (such as Parmesan or pecorino)

- 2 cloves of garlic, finely chopped

- Fresh parsley, chopped

- Salt and pepper (to taste)

- 400g ground chicken breast

- 1 egg

- 2 tablespoons of breadcrumbs (or rolled oats for a gluten-free version)

- Extra virgin olive oil (for cooking).

For the tomato sauce:

- 2 cloves of garlic, finely chopped

- Fresh basil, chopped

- Salt and pepper (to taste)

- 400g of peeled tomatoes, chopped

- 1 onion, finely chopped

- Extra virgin olive oil.

Directions:

1. Make the meatballs: In a bowl, mix the ground chicken breast with the egg, breadcrumbs, grated cheese, minced garlic, and fresh parsley.
2. Add salt and pepper to taste. Mix the ingredients well until you get a homogeneous mixture.

3. Shape Meatballs: Take some of the chicken mixture and shape into small meatballs with your hands. Make sure they are all similar in size for even cooking.
4. Cooking the meatballs: Heat a little extra virgin olive oil in a non-stick pan over medium-high heat.
5. Place the meatballs in the pan and cook them for about 8-10 minutes, turning them gently, until they are golden brown and cooked through.
6. Make the tomato sauce: In a separate pan, heat some extra virgin olive oil and add the chopped onion and garlic.
7. Saute until soft and lightly browned. Add the chopped peeled tomatoes, fresh basil, salt and pepper. Cook the sauce over medium-low heat for about 15-20 minutes, stirring occasionally.

8. Service: Pour the hot tomato sauce onto a serving platter and arrange the chicken balls on top.
9. You can garnish with fresh basil leaves. Serve the meatballs with tomato sauce as an appetizer or as a main course, accompanied by vegetables or a fresh salad.
10. Chicken meatballs with tomato sauce are a tasty and protein dish suitable for the Dukan diet. Be sure to cook the meatballs over medium-high heat for a crispy surface, but check that they are cooked through on the inside.
11. The tomato sauce adds flavor and moisture to the meatballs. You can customize the recipe by adding spices or herbs to the meatball mixture, such as oregano or parsley.

Chicken Supreme

Ingredients:

- ½ glass of white wine
- 1 tbsp fat-free yogurt
- ½ tsp chives, chopped
- Salt, to taste
- ½ chicken breast, sliced
- ½ tsp Dijon mustard
- Pepper, to taste

Directions:

1. In a pan, dry fry the sliced chicken pieces.
2. Add white wine to the pan and continue cooking, till the chicken is completely cooked.

3. Mix the mustard, yogurt, chives, salt and pepper in a separate bowl in order to achieve a sauce-like consistency.
4. Once the chicken has cooled, add the sauce to it.

Baked Egg Custard

Ingredients:

- 2 tbsp sweetener
- 1 tsp almond extract
- ½ tbsp vanilla essence
- 3 eggs
- 2 egg whites
- 3 cups skimmed milk
- Pinch of salt

Directions:

1. Preheat oven at 275 °F.
2. Boil the milk – keep stirring so it does not stick to the bottom of the container.

3. Stir sweetener and salt, till they totally dissolve.
4. In a bowl, beat the eggs. Then add almond extract and vanilla essence. Add the hot milk while still beating the mixture.
5. Pour equal quantities of this mixture into ramekins. Place them in a pan – and pour boiling water till half the height of the ramekin.
6. Bake for about an hour, till the custards become firm in the edges.
7. Let it cool then refrigerate.

Chicken Nuggets

Ingredients:

- 1 teaspoon paprika

- 1 teaspoon garlic powder

- Salt and pepper to taste

- 2 chicken breasts

- 2 tablespoons of 0% fat Greek yogurt

- Juice of half a lemon

- Basil leaves for garnish (optional)

Directions:

1. Cut the chicken breasts into bite-sized pieces. In a bowl, mix Greek yogurt, lemon juice,

paprika, garlic powder, salt, and pepper to create a marinade.
2. Add the chicken bites to the marinade and mix well to coat them evenly. Let marinate for at least 15 minutes.
3. Heat a nonstick skillet over medium-high heat. Add the marinated chicken bites to the skillet and cook for 10 to 12 minutes or until golden brown and fully cooked through.
4. Garnish with basil leaves (if desired). Serve the chicken bites hot.

Hard-Boiled Eggs Cut In Half And Seasoned With Herbs

Ingredients:

- Basil, chives) finely chopped

- Salt and pepper (optional)

- 4 eggs

- Aromatic herbs (such as parsley,

Directions:

1. Put the eggs in a pot and cover with cold water. Bring the water to a boil and let the eggs cook for 10 minutes.
2. Drain the eggs and cool them under cold running water. Shell the eggs and cut them in half. Season the eggs with the chopped herbs.

3. Add salt and pepper to taste, if desired. Serve the seasoned hard-boiled eggs as an appetizer.

Chocolate Ice Cream Dukan Style

Ingredients:

- A drop of vanilla extract

- 6 tsp granulated sweetener

- 3 pieces eggs

- 2 tsp reduced fat cocoa powder

- 350 grams fat-free from age frays

Directions:

1. Whisk up the egg whites with the use of an electronic whisk until they come to the stiff peak stage. Place in the sweetener and combine entirely with the use of a spoon.
2. With the use of a fork, beat the egg yolks and then pour them over the egg white mixture. Gently stir the mixture.

3. Add in the from age frays, vanilla extract and cocoa powder to the egg mixture and fold in.
4. Pour the resulting mixture into an ice cream maker and churn until it turns into a soft ice cream. This should take about 20 minutes.
5. Serve immediately or keep in the freezer for about a week.

Prawn Cocktail Dukan-Style

Ingredients:

- 1 tbsp chives (chopped)

- A pinch of paprika

- 200 grams 0 percent Greek yogurt

- Tabasco sauce (optional)

- A squeeze of lemon juice

- 150 grams cocktail prawns (cooked)

Directions:

1. In a medium-sized bowl, place the Greek yogurt, lemon juice, Tabasco sauce, paprika and chopped chives. Use a hand blender to combine all ingredients thoroughly.

2. Place in the refrigerator and serve chilled on the side of the cooked cocktail prawns.

www.ingramcontent.com/pod-product-compliance
Lightning Source LLC
LaVergne TN
LVHW010224070526
838199LV00062B/4712